Pee Happy:

A No Non-Sense Approach to Potty Training Even the Most Stubborn Child

Minute Help Guides

Minute Help Press

www.minutehelp.com

Cover Image:

© Serhiy Kobyakov - Fotolia.com

Table of Contents

When and How to Begin Potty Training

For most children, potty training is the first time they have to actively exert control over their own bodily functions. The process can be stressful for both children and parents, especially if it's rushed into too early. Rather than a single event in a child's life, potty training should be viewed as a process that can take anywhere from a few months to a year. Before beginning potty training, parents should ensure that their child is ready, both emotionally and physiologically, to start the process.

Pre-Potty Training

Using the toilet is second nature to adults, so it's easy to forget how intimidating potty training can be for young children. There is much you can do to prevent anxiety about potty training. Before your child begins formal toilet training, work on getting him accustomed to the sounds and sights of the bathroom.

Beginning when your child can sit up on his own, usually around six months of age, have him sit on the floor near you when you are using the bathroom. Young children love imitating their parents, and if your child is used to seeing adults using the toilet, he will gradually begin to want to do it himself.

Beginning around eight months, talk to your child about bodily functions before changing his diaper. Children begin understanding language long before they can actually use it. A child who has heard his parents talk about bodily functions will typically understand these functions long before other children. If you see your child straining to poop, ask her, "Are you pooping?" Marking the exact moment at which your child relieves his bowels and bladder will, over the course of several months, help him begin to recognize feelings of fullness long before he is ready to begin potty training.

Around your child's first birthday, begin placing him on the toilet or a training potty immediately after changing her diaper. This teaches him to associate going to the bathroom with using the toilet. Be sure to always hold him to prevent him from flailing and hitting his head or falling into the toilet. Negative early experiences with the bathroom can dramatically increase the time and effort required to potty train your child.

Whenever your child appears to be straining to use the bathroom, immediately place him on the toilet. If he poops or pees in the toilet, lavish him with praise and encourage him to delight in this impressive accomplishment.

Perhaps most importantly, ensure that your child always has a clean diaper. Children instinctively dislike the feeling of sitting in a wet diaper, but if your child becomes accustomed to this sensation he will be unbothered by it. This can dramatically stunt potty training. When you allow your child to sit in a wet diaper, even for a few minutes, you are training him to not care about cleanliness or hygiene, a dangerous precedent for when you begin actual potty training.

Potty Training Readiness

In her book *The Cultural Nature of Human Development*, developmental psychologist Barbara Rogoff points to a number of potty training practices around the world. In some tribal societies, children never use diapers and quickly learn to control their bowels and bladders. In some societies, children are forcibly potty trained between six months and a year. While these early potty training anecdotes can seem impressive and even shocking, the methods used by these societies are impractical for most Western parents. Potty training in the first year of life frequently requires parents to tolerate substantial messes. Children living in these societies frequently use corners and outdoor areas and never have to use the toilet, eliminating one common obstacle to potty training.

Unlike these children, children living in Western societies have to master several different skills to use the toilet. First, they must have full awareness of their bowels and bladder. Second, they must be able to articulate that they need to use the potty and must have the physical skills necessary to climb onto a toilet or training potty. Consequently, pediatricians and child experts frequently talk about "potty training readiness." These are the skills a child must have before he can competently begin the process of potty training. To be truly ready to take on potty training, your child must be able to the things listed below.

Physical Skills

- Children should be able to walk and run steadily without falling down. This correlates strongly with the degree of physical control required to control their bladder and bowels. Competent walking and running also ensures that your child will be able to safely climb onto and sit down on a toilet.
- Babies and toddlers should regularly go three to four hours with a dry diaper before commencing potty training. Very young

children frequently urinate small amounts every few minutes, and it is impractical to expect these children to begin potty training.

- Children should give some signal that they are pooping such as grunting, turning red or going to a corner. This indicates that children are aware of their bodily processes, and without this awareness, children can't master potty training.

Cognitive and Behavioral Skills

- Children must be able to pull their pants down and up. Your child doesn't need to be able to zip or button his own pants, but he should be able to undress himself enough to use the bathroom without assistance.
- Potty training readiness requires that children have enough verbal skills to follow simple directions such as, "Hand me that toy" or, "Throw that in the trash." While children don't necessarily need to be speaking to be potty trained, children with strong verbal skills can master potty training more quickly. When toddlers begin speaking in two and three-word sentences, they are more likely to be successful at potty training.
- Your child must be able to sit quietly for two to five minutes. This skill frequently comes

and goes during the toddler years, so choose a period during which your child is being cooperative and calm to begin potty training.

- Children must be eager to please their parents and understand the concept of rules to begin potty training. If your child can understand words such as no, please and yes, he may be ready to begin potty training.
- A desire for independence is key to mastering toilet skills. If your child is resistant to getting help, imitates the adults around him and often wants to do things himself, she'll be better-equipped to master potty training.

Perhaps most importantly, your child must not be resistant to potty training. Forcing a fearful or rebellious child to begin potty training can backfire. Wait until your child shows an interest in using the potty. If he resists training, wait a few weeks and try again.

Potty Training Methods

There are a variety of potty training methods available, with practitioners of each claiming that their method is the best. The truth is that there's no miracle method that will make potty training easy and accident-free. Instead, potty training requires patience and children must feel rewarded for their efforts. Each individual potty training method has benefits and drawbacks, so you should choose the approach – or combination of approaches – that best suits your child and your family's needs.

Pediatrician T. Berry Brazelton likes to point out that no child is still using diapers in her teenage years. Children all eventually learn to use the potty, no matter how frustrating the process is for parents and no matter how long it takes. Thus parents should draw the lesson that potty training will not last forever and that there is no one perfect method. Parents can have success using a variety of different methods and even by combining potty training styles.

However, for the fastest and most stress-free results, parents should strive for consistency. Your child should, after a few days of potty training, be able to predict how you will react to accidents and to successes. This allows your child to actively choose to become potty trained, and the control a child feels over the process is strongly correlated to potty training success. Although you can combine a number of the below styles, avoid using approaches that conflict with one another or that prescribe vastly different reactions to accidents, setbacks and other common potty training dilemmas. Your child may end up profoundly confused and resistant to learning to use the toilet. Developmental psychologists, pediatricians and other child experts have studied the effectiveness of potty training methods for generations, and the overwhelming consensus is that the specific method used is much less important than a parent's commitment to consistency.

Diaper Free

Diaper-free parenting is among the most controversial parenting choices, but it is an effective potty training style. Although there are several different approaches, including diapering only at night, never using diapers or stopping the use of diapers when the baby hits 6 months, the common theme with all diaper-free methods is that not using diapers makes it easier for parents to predict when their children will need to use the bathroom. During the first several months of life, parents simply wipe up any messes. When their babies are able to sit up, they begin placing babies on the toilet or training potty.

If you are interested in trying diaper-free potty training, place absorbent towels in areas your baby frequents. Then leave his diaper off all day, every day. Carefully observe his behavior before and immediately after he urinates or has a bowel movement. Once you've established the behaviors he exhibits prior to going, begin placing him on the toilet when he makes his potty face or displays other behaviors indicating he needs to go.

Benefits

This is the potty training method that has been used, with slight variation, throughout most of human history, so it has a long and successful track record. Parents interested in more natural parenting approaches will find it especially appealing. It saves parents substantial money on diapers and typically results in children who are potty trained much earlier than children who used any other method.

Drawbacks

Diaper-free parenting can get extraordinarily messy and requires near-constant attention to your child. It is a highly stigmatized practice that friends and family may not understand.

When to Use It

This method only works if started very early. If your child is older than 6 months or so, it's likely too late to implement diaper-free training. But if you have a young baby and would like to try diaper-free training, start by experimenting with an hour or two without a diaper and work up to progressively more time.

Who it Works For

Because this method is used before babies have developed a strong personality or verbal skills, it can work for virtually any child. Parents who are self-conscious or uncomfortable explaining parenting choices to friends and family are unlikely to enjoy using this method. One parent or competent caregiver such as a nanny must be able to be with the baby at all times and should be able to recognize the signs that the baby is about to urinate or have a bowel movement.

The Practice Method

This method is an outstanding introduction to potty training and teaches children to recognize the signs of a full bladder. It also helps kids get used to sitting on the potty. This method is safe to use even on children who aren't emotionally or physically ready for potty training, and some parents do it with infants as young as six months old.

To use this method, place your child on the potty 5 to 10 times a day at regular intervals. If he goes to the bathroom, reward him for his efforts with a hug, sticker, a small treat or other form of positive attention. To properly institute this method, you must allow your child to practice using the potty every day, and must provide him enough opportunities to use the potty that, if timed right and if he masters potty training, he can do all of his eliminative functions on the toilet.

Benefits

The practice method requires only a small time commitment and is unlikely to stress your child. Because it is completely reward-based, it encourages your child to develop a positive association with using the potty. Children who are eager to master potty training may be able to be potty trained using only this method.

Drawbacks

This approach will typically need to be combined with another method after your child becomes comfortable using the potty. It is unlikely to work with stubborn children and requires that parents keep a fairly rigid schedule of practice sessions.

When to Use It

This style of potty training is best used as an introduction to potty training in very young children. Start using it when your child is old enough to sit on the potty and understand simple directions. Children whose parents use this method early and who then switch to another method are frequently potty trained earlier than other children.

Who It Works For

Parents with busy, unpredictable schedules may find this approach overly rigid and scheduled because it requires frequent trips to the potty with a child who may not need to go. Children who are resistant to potty training are unlikely to relish this method. However, children who love imitating adults, who are eager to please and who are able to sit still for one to two minutes can quickly master potty training using this approach.

Brazelton Method

This approach, which is endorsed by the American Academy of Pediatrics and which has been around for decades, was developed by Dr. T. Berry Brazelton. Brazelton argues that potty training is a developmental milestone that children will reach on their own when they are exposed to a supportive, nurturing environment.

Dr. Brazelton recommends waiting until a child shows all the signs of potty training readiness and is interested in and willing to try potty training. When this occurs, parents should begin leaving children's diapers off during the day. Gently encourage your child to use the potty throughout the day and reward her when she goes to the toilet. As children learn to control their bladders and bowels during the day, they will slowly master nighttime control. Brazelton advocates leaving children in diapers at night until they are able to remain dry almost all nights. This, he says, takes substantially longer than daytime training because it requires nonconscious bladder control. Children are never punished for accidents in the Brazelton system and are lavished with praise for their efforts and positive results.

Benefits

Brazelton's approach is unlikely to provoke power struggles or tantrums. Its endorsement by the American Academy of Pediatrics can help reassure parents who are anxious about potty training, and it allows parents to delay potty training without guilt if their children are not ready.

Drawbacks

The average age for potty training using this method is three, creating an obstacle for parents whose children must start preschool. Diaper-free days can be messy without careful supervision.

When to Use It

Brazelton advises that, if children do not show all of the signs of potty training readiness by the age of three, parents can begin at this time. Before your child is ready for the Brazelton method, it can be helpful to talk to her about basic bodily functions and to allow her to see you using the toilet.

Who It Works For

This method is effective with a wide variety of children, but can be especially useful with children who are resistant to potty training or for whom another method has failed. Parents who are able to provide supervision and encouragement during diaper-free days are more likely to have positive results with this method.

Reward-Based Methods

Many potty training approaches incorporate rewards of some kind. A child might get a sticker on a star chart each time he uses the potty or be promised a special reward when he completes potty training. The American Academy of Pediatrics has pointed out that punishment can cause negative behaviors but that children are often highly responsive to reward-based approaches. Your child must show signs of potty training readiness before you begin using this method, and you must choose a reward that will give your child a strong incentive to complete potty training.

Tell your child in advance that every time he uses the potty he will get a special reward. Because children use the bathroom so frequently during the day, stickers to keep or to place on a chart to trade in for a bigger prize are often good choices. Then, every time your child uses the potty, praise him and give him the reward. Never punish accidents. Simply clean them up without comment.

Benefits

This method turns potty training into a positive achievement, with each day consisting of little victories. It can help both parents and children feel more positive about potty training and encourage parent-child closeness during the potty training process. Reward-based methods can also be combined with other potty training approaches. Importantly, rewards must be implemented at the same time every time. For example, if you give a child a sticker five minutes after using the potty one time, you should not wait an hour next time.

Drawbacks

No matter how well you institute this system, if your child is not emotionally and physiologically ready for potty training, it won't work. Reward-based systems also require that your child have strong enough verbal skills to understand the concept of a reward. The delayed gratification used in reward-based systems is confusing to some children.

When to Use It

If your child has gotten rewards before and understands the concept, he's probably mature enough to use a reward-based system. To work properly, you must use this system consistently. You can't, for example, reward using the potty during the day but not at night. Every small victory should get your child a sticker, a stamp or some other indicator of success.

Who It Works For

This method can be used with all children who have basic verbal skills. Children with developmental delays may struggle to understand this method, but can still use it if rewards are implemented consistently.

Every 15 Minutes Method

This approach works exactly the way it sounds. Parents place their child on the toilet every fifteen minutes over the course of several days. While this strategy might sound exhausting, it is also highly effective. Few children can go to the bathroom more frequently than every 15 minutes, so the result of this strategy is that children are quickly using the toilet every time they need to go to the bathroom. After a few hours or days of this, your child will quickly get into the habit of going in the potty. Getting used to using the potty also makes it more likely that children will find dirty diapers uncomfortable and unacceptable, giving them a strong incentive to control their bowels and bladders.

If you want to try this method, consider doing so on a weekend. For the first 4 hours, put your child on the toilet every fifteen minutes. If he does not go every time, switch to every 20 minutes for the fifth hour and every 25 for the sixth, continuing to add five minutes every hour until you've reached what seems to be a comfortable potty schedule for your child. Continue placing your child on the potty at this interval for the remainder of a weekend. Then encourage him to go to the potty himself when he needs to. After a day or two of the 15 minute method, your child will have likely learned what it feels like to need to go to the bathroom and will be mostly potty trained.

Benefits

This method works quickly and is ideal for parents who need their children potty trained in time to start preschool or to visit relatives. It's also unlikely to provoke resistance from the child because children don't have accidents and other frustrations using this method. There are no messes to clean up and no accidents to worry about. There's also no long-term planning required.

Drawbacks

Most parents find this method truly exhausting. Hyper children with little self-control are unlikely to benefit from it. They will see the time spent on the potty as something that takes away from having fun, which can cause them to develop a negative association with potty training.

One Day Training

Different versions of one day potty training have been around for several decades. Each variation focuses on developing muscle memory for using the toilet. Muscle memory is the immediate, unthinking tendency to adopt a particular stance or movement, and is an important part of potty training. Early one day training methods tended to be punitive in nature, but the American Academy of Pediatrics advises against such methods. Punishment can create fear about using the potty, which can make the process longer and more frustrating for both parent and child.

A newer one day method has been popularized by talk show host Dr. Phil. In this version, children practice with a doll, reward the doll for mastering potty training and then practice potty training themselves.

To implement this method, get your child a drink and wet doll. The best choice is an anatomically correct doll, because children will relate more to a doll who looks like them and are better able to understand the process when the doll's potty training is realistic. Thus boys should have male dolls and girls should have female dolls. Encourage your child to help the doll use the potty and then reward the doll for doing so. When the doll is potty trained, throw a "potty party" for the doll and tell your child she will get a potty party for finishing potty training too. Next, give her lots of liquids to increase her need to go to the potty and take her to the potty every few minutes. If she has an accident, take her to the potty, pull down her pants and have her sit down 5 to 10 times in a row. This helps her develop muscle memory and establishes a strong correlation between urination and using the potty. When your child is successfully using the potty nine times out of every ten, throw her a potty party. Give her a cake, balloons and a special present.

Benefits

When children show all of the signs of potty training readiness, this method really can work in a day or two. It is especially useful for parents who don't have weeks to commit to potty training or who need their children to learn to use the potty quickly for school, a vacation or day care. It also helps normalize the process of potty training through the use of the doll, eliminating any shame or embarrassment your child might feel about bodily functions.

Drawbacks

Drink and wet dolls potty immediately after getting fluids, but real people experience a delay. This can be confusing to some children, making the doll an imperfect model. Additionally, repeatedly putting your child on a potty can feel like a punishment to some children. The approach does not directly teach potty training for bowel movements, but most children are better able to predict and control their bowels than their bladders.

When to Use It

In addition to showing all the standard signs of potty training readiness, children must have strong verbal skills and understand pretend play. The method generally works best for children older than two. Begin training on a low-stress day, when your child is in a cooperative mood and when there are no distractions such as company or illness.

Who It Works For

Children who have difficulty with empathy, including children with developmental delays such as autism and Asperger's syndrome are unlikely to respond to this method. Most other children will readily learn potty training using the one day method.

Parent-Led Potty Training

This method is actually a combination of several other potty training styles, but differs from Brazelton's child-led training in that the parent determines the timing of potty training. This is a slower approach than some other methods, but tends to be lower stress for both parent and child.

To try parent-led potty training, purchase a potty chair and "big kid" underwear for your child. Begin by having your child sit on the potty chair fully clothed and talk to him about using the potty. After he's become comfortable sitting on the potty, have him sit on the potty chair without his pants on. Next, put him in underwear instead of diapers and take him to the potty chair every hour or so and encourage him to go to the bathroom. If he successfully goes in the potty chair, lavish him with praise or give him a small reward. Continue encouraging your child to use the potty for several weeks and keep him in underwear when he is at home and closely supervised. When you go out in public, put him in training underwear or diapers and offer frequent trips to the bathroom. At bedtime, have him use the potty and wake him up once or twice at night to go potty.

Benefits

This method, unlike some others, does not require intensive, concentrated effort and can instead be implemented gradually over the course of several weeks. This makes it an ideal choice for busy parents. It is also less likely to produce potty training resistance than some other methods because children aren't expected to produce rapid results.

Drawbacks

Frequent accidents are common using this approach, and it can take several months for children to become fully potty trained. Parent-led potty training is also less specific than other methods. There's no set program or schedule, so parents may be left feeling uncertain about what specifically to do to help their children.

When to Use It

This method is dependent on the parent's schedule, and parents can implement it whenever they are ready for their children to become potty trained. It requires fewer verbal skills than some other methods, but does still require basic potty training readiness. Parents should generally avoid implementing this method until their children are at least 18 months old.

Who it Works For

This method can be used with almost all children, including kids with developmental and cognitive delays. It works by developing strong habits and correlations, so children don't necessarily need to understand the potty training process to successfully become potty trained.

Underwear Only Potty Training

This method is used for older children who have not been successfully potty trained using other methods. Occasionally referred to as independent potty training or self-directed potty training, it encourages children to take responsibility for their own bodies and hygiene. This method should not be used unless your child can speak in full and complete sentences and fully understands the concept of using the potty.

To implement this method, purchase underwear featuring your child's favorite characters, then tell your child, "They don't like to be dirty." Take away her diapers or training pants during the day and allow her to wear her underwear. Ask her frequently if she needs to use the potty, but don't force her to do so. If she has an accident, help her clean up the mess without commenting on the accident or becoming angry, then put her in a fresh pair of underwear. Children quickly learn that it's uncomfortable to have accidents in big kid underwear. Because older children already understand the basics of using the potty, this encourages your child to potty train herself over the course of several weeks.

Benefits

When other methods have failed, this method can be highly effective. It also requires little monitoring of your child and allows her to develop a sense of independence and control over her own body. For parents who have been stuck waging potty training wars for months, it can be a welcome relief from the constant stress and power struggles.

Drawbacks

This method is unlikely to work on children under four. If your child does not have a full range of verbal skills and has not already been exposed to the process of potty training, it won't work and can increase potty training resistance. It is also messy and requires parents and children to frequently clean up accidents.

When to Use It

If your child has been resistant to other potty training methods, take a two week hiatus from potty training and then implement this method. Don't try self-directed potty training when you have company, when your child is starting school or at other times that an accident could embarrass her. Humiliation can increase your child's resistance to potty training.

Who it Works For

This method will not work for children with developmental delays that interfere with verbal skills and following directions. Older children with a full understanding of potty training and strong verbal skills are most likely to be successful. You must have time to stay home with your child and allow her to make her own mistakes without passing judgment or becoming angry. If you have been frustrated or angered by the potty training process, avoid using this method until you've calmed down enough to avoid taking out your frustration on your child.

Naked Method

This approach is commonly called the "Naked and $75 Method" because it's likely you'll have to spend money to get your carpets cleaned. It is essentially a version of the diaper-free method designed for older children. This method works by making children intensely aware of their bodily functions. To implement it, simply allow your child to spend three to five days completely naked, encouraging him to use the potty frequently. Your child will know when he's had an accident, which can help him develop a strong correlation between needing to go and using the potty. As with other methods, never punish your child for having an accident. Simply clean up any mistakes in a matter of fact manner without becoming angry.

Benefits

This method helps children understand the exact moment at which they go potty, which can be difficult for some children. When implemented correctly and without punishment, it can help your child become completely potty trained in only a few days.

Drawbacks

This is one of the few potty training methods that has not proven consistently successful in scientific studies. In addition to being messy, it can also be highly stressful for both parents and children. Additionally, some children may continue to soil themselves in clothes because they only understand what it feels like to have an accident when naked.

When to Use It

This method is best used in combination with other methods. Consider allowing your child to be naked while implementing a reward-based method. As with other methods, your child must show all the signs of potty training readiness. However, it is possible to implement this method slightly earlier than other methods. Children eighteen months and older may be able to master potty training using this approach.

Who it Works For

Children and parents who are uncomfortable with bodily functions will find this method humiliating and stressful. But if you can adopt a laid back approach to your child's accidents and turn naked days into fun days, this method may be ideal.

Other Potty Training Considerations

No matter which potty training method you choose to use, having the right supplies and right attitude can greatly affect your child's success. Avoid rushing into potty training. Instead, you should carefully weigh your options for several weeks before approaching your child about potty training. Make sure the right supplies are readily available and that you're prepared to commit several weeks to the process.

Potty Training During Transitions

Children frequently regress during times of stress or transition. If you've just had a new baby or moved, your child may begin acting younger than he actually is. This is not a good time to begin potty training and decreases your child's likelihood of potty training success. Instead, wait till he has adapted to his new surroundings.

Potty Training Supplies

The right supplies can make potty training easier for both you and your child. Make sure you have a comfortable training potty available for your child to use. Consider allowing your child to pick the potty she likes best. Many companies offer brightly-colored potties featuring favorite children's characters. While it may seem silly, spending a few extra dollars on a potty your child loves can encourage her to actually use the potty.

Have plenty of baby wipes and diaper rash ointment on hand at all times. This makes cleaning up accidents easy and prevents your child from developing skin problems caused by accidents. If you're using a potty training method that makes accidents particularly likely, consider moving your child's toys to a floor without carpet and encouraging him to play in this room to decrease messes.

The right underwear and training pants can make a huge difference. Allow your child to select nighttime training pants. This underwear is more absorbent than cotton underwear, but still allows your child to feel wet, making it a better choice for potty training than diapers. Similarly, your child should be allowed to select cotton underwear to wear during the day. Never yell at or punish her for soiling this underwear, but encourage her to keep these special big kid pants clean.

Potty Training and Vocabulary

Use the proper terms for your child's genitals and body parts. This serves several purposes. First, it increases her vocabulary and helps her communicate with teachers, grandparents and other caregivers. Second, teaching the right words instead of cutesy words teaches children that pottying is just like any other bodily function and not something of which to be ashamed. Young children are immensely curious about their bodies, and when they feel like they can trust their parents to provide them with accurate information, they are more likely to rely on their parents. This reliance increases potty training success. It also makes it easier for your child to communicate with you in an emergency. If your child knows the proper name for body parts, he can tell you exactly where it hurts. Knowing proper terms for genitals is an important part of development, and can also increase your embarrassment about bodies. This makes it much easier for you to talk to your child about his body throughout his childhood, not just during potty training.

Medical Issues

Before beginning potty training, consult your child's pediatrician to ensure that potty training is developmentally appropriate. If you experience difficulty with potty training, get a complete physical for your child ebfore determining that he is just being stubborn. Delays in genital development and some health problems can cause difficulty with potty training.

Completion of potty training does not necessarily mean your child will be able to take care of his body by himself. Childre tend to need hel wiping after a bowel movement for a year or two after potty training. Girls should be taught to wipe front to back to avoid inadvertently sweeping fecal matter into the vagina. Teaching your child this important skill can help her avoid urinary tract and yeast infections.

Nighttime Accidents

It's common for children to continue having nighttime accidents up until age five or so. This is not due to stubbornness or failure to be potty trained. Instead, young children tend to sleep more deeply and have smaller bladders. Consider allowing your child to sleep in training pants. Avoid giving her fluids just before bedtime and wake her up to go to the bathroom at night. Bedwetting typically goes away on its own by the time children start school, but if the problem continues, consult your child's pediatrician.

Parental Attitude

Most of us are raised with a sense of shame and embarrassment about urination, defecation and genitals. This shame, however, has no place in potty training. Never teach your child that her genitals are dirty or shameful. This not only stunts potty traininig, but can also cause a host of problems in adulthood. Treat potty training the same way you would treat the process of learning any other skill such as reading, writing or eating solid foods. When children view potty training as a fun skill they must master rather than a source of humiliation, they catch on much more quickly.

Modeling Potty Training

Children benefit greatly from watching their parents use the toilet. It helps using the potty seem like a grown-up task, and young children want nothing more than to be like grown-ups. It's especially important for children to see their same-sex parent using the potty. This teaches proper hygiene and helps them relate to the process of using the potty much more than using a doll or watching the opposite sex parent use the potty will.

What to Do About the Stubborn Child

Potty training resistance occurs when a child who understands the use of the bathroom and who is capable of controlling his bowels and bladder actively resists toilet training. These children are incredibly frustrating for many parents, especially since many of them are older children who have not yet mastered using the bathroom. When parents get frustrated, they tend to lash out or become more controlling with potty training, which can result in even more resistance from the child. If you're experiencing these difficulties with your child, step back and take a week off from potty training before doing anything else. This can help to "reset" any errors you've made in training your child and make your child more receptive to the process.

Is Your Child Really Being Stubborn?

Parents sometimes confuse stubbornness with something else. The truth is that most children do not resist potty training once they are old enough to understand the process and if they are given a supportive environment in which to learn. Potty training resistance is really about power. The child is locked in a power struggle with the parent and it's usually because of something the parent has done wrong. Behaviors that can increase stubbornness and cause potty training resistance include:

- Punishing your child for accidents.
- Forcing your child to be potty trained before he shows all the signs of readiness.
- Rushing through the process of potty training.
- Instilling shame in your child about bodily processes by referring to bodily fluids as gross or disgusting.
- Creating a bathroom environment that is not accessible to the child because the toilet is too high, the room is too cold, etc.
- Making your child use the bathroom alone when he is scared.

- Telling too many people in your child's life about potty training.
- Encouraging older siblings, family and friends to goad a child into potty training; this can embarrass the child and cause him to back out of the process.
- Offering rewards for potty training that you never actually give.
- Threatening your child by telling him he has to go live with another family if he's not potty trained or that the monster will get him if he has accidents.

If you've done any of these things, the first step is to apologize to your child and promise never to do them again. Take a break from potty training and say nothing about accidents, diaper changes or anything potty-related to your child.

Fear, anxiety and distraction can also closely resemble stubbornness. Some children are afraid of the toilet or of the bathroom. Others feel so much pressure to use the bathroom on command that they withhold their stool until no one is watching. Hyperactive children who are prone to distraction may struggle with potty training because they are

Symptoms of the Stubborn Child

Some children simply master potty training more easily than others. If you haven't made any of the mistakes listed above, it is possible that your child is simply learning more slowly than some kids do. Very bright, engaging and well-behaved children can all experience difficulties with potty training. But for some children, potty training becomes a battleground because they have learned that they can use toilet training to exercise control over their parents and obtain attention. Some symptoms of potty training resistance include:

- Holding in bowel movements and urine while sitting on the corner and then hiding in a corner to go in a diaper.
- Verbalizing a refusal to be potty trained.
- Holding in stools long enough to become constipated.
- Showing little interest in rewards for successful attempts at using the toilet.

- Telling you their diaper is dirty but refusing to try using the potty.
- Peeing or pooping in his pants when he is angry or frustrated with you.
- Complete refusal to ever use the potty, despite seeming uncomfortable when his pants or diaper is dirty.

Strategies for the Stubborn Child

How you deal with the stubborn child depends upon the child's age, personality and cognitive abilities. In children under 4, the best response to stubbornness is to abandon potty training for a few weeks and then try again. While this advice might not be what frustrated parents want to hear, forcing potty training on a child who is resistant and unready can dramatically prolong the process.

Take a Break

Give your child a complete break from potty training. Tell him you can see that he's not ready and you're not going to push the process on him. If you've taken any coercive measures to potty train him, apologize. Then go at least two weeks without mentioning potty training, complaining about changing diapers or reading any potty books to your child. This allows your child a blank slate on which to begin again in a few weeks.

Talk to Your Child

Many parents simply assume their children are being stubborn without ever asking the child why he is resisting training. After a hiatus from potty training, ask your child if there's anything you can do to make potty training better for him. He may point to several things you are doing that are upsetting him and, if this is the case, honor his requests for changes in the way you potty train. You might also find that small adjustments can help the process. Large toilets, cold bathrooms and the sound of toilets flushing are frequently frightening obstacles to young children. If you can mitigate these problems by, for example, using a training potty, warming up the bathroom or allowing your child to leave the toilet unflushed until he adjusts to the noise, do so.

Avoid Rewarding the Wrong Behavior

Parents sometimes inadvertently reward the precise behaviors they don't want to see in their children. Avoid reacting to your child's provocative behavior about potty training. To some children, negative attention is just as good as any other attention. And for other children, when they upset their parents they learn that they can control and manipulate adults, so they continue the problematic behavior.

Give Your Child Control

You may feel like your child is controlling your entire family with his stubborn refusal to become potty trained. But the truth is that when children feel like they are really in control, they are unlikely to resist their parents' potty training efforts. Whatever you do, don't engage in power struggles with your child, and honor his wishes. For example, if he doesn't want other people watching him using the potty, listen to this request. By handing control back to your child, you decrease his incentive to try to turn potty training into a battle of wills.

Potty Training Older Children

Most children are potty trained between the ages of 3 and 4 in the United States. Although the average age of potty training has crept up over the past few decades, there is still a huge stigma associated with late potty training. If your preschooler is not yet potty trained, friends and family may make harsh comments about your parents and may even judge your child. Many preschools do not allow children who are not fully potty trained, and some pediatricians assume that late potty training constitutes neglect.

The truth is that there are a variety of reasons kids end up being potty trained late, and there is no scientific evidence that there are any long term effects of potty training. Family stress, toilet training resistance and individual personalities can all result in late potty training. However, because of the social stigma associated with preschoolers who aren't yet potty trained, it's important to take special care to avoid humiliating your child. This means that only people who need to know about your child's potty training status should know. Avoid spreading the word to friends and distant family, and never make fun of your child because he is not yet potty trained.

Oops! We Forgot to Potty Train!

In a busy world, it's easy to put off potty training for months until you wake up and realize you have a four-year-old who is not yet able to use the potty. If you haven't started potty training with your child yet, you don't need to take any special measures just because your child is older. Simply choose a potty training method that works for your family's needs and begin implementing it.

My Child Keeps Having Accidents at Night!

Nighttime accidents are common well into the school years. In fact, pediatricians typically consider children potty trained even if they continue to wet the bed nightly. Children's urethras are narrower than adults', and they have smaller bladders and sleep more deeply. These factors combine to make nighttime potty training substantially more difficult than daytime potty training. Before changing your child's nighttime routine, get your child a complete physical. Some congenital conditions can make nighttime accidents more common, and urinary tract infections often account for nighttime bedwetting. If your doctor has given your child a clean bill of health, try the following:

- Withhold all fluids for an hour before bed, and make sure your child uses the bathroom just before she goes to sleep. This ensures that her bladder is completely empty.
- Line your child's bed with rubber sheets. This decreases staining and is also more likely to help her wake up if she has an accident. When children wake up immediately after having an accident, it's easier for them to gradually gain nighttime bladder control.

- Wake your child up two to three times at night to go to the bathroom. Even if he doesn't go, this helps him to be more aware of his bladder at night and increases the likelihood that he'll begin waking himself up.
- Put your child in nighttime training pants. These pants are designed to help your child feel wet, which will help him wake up if he has an accident. They also decrease messes and help your child feel less embarrassed about nighttime accidents.

My Child Was Potty Trained and Now He's Not

Children frequently regress after the birth of a new sibling, during a move or if their parents are experiencing marital difficulties. If your child has suddenly begun having accidents again, the problem is not a potty training issue at all. Instead, the key is to focus on helping your child manage his stress without putting pressure on him to return to potty training. Spend extra time with him and talk to him about how he is feeling. If, after several weeks, the situation has not improved, begin potty training again. If your child is still having trouble, consult your pediatrician for a referral to a qualified child behavioral therapist who can help your child cope with his feelings.

My Child Refuses to Be Potty Trained

When older children are resistant to potty training, parents can quickly become extremely frustrated. By the age of four, children are old enough to understand the concept of using the toilet and to exercise control over their bladders during the day. If you've tried several potty training methods and they haven't worked, or if your child has flat-out told you he doesn't care about potty training, it's time to change strategies. After consulting your doctor to ensure there are no underlying medical or psychological conditions, abandon all potty training efforts for two weeks. This may seem counterintuitive, but it gives both you and your child a break from the stress of training. Then tell your child that there are two new household rules. First, big kids can't go out with dirty pants and second, big kids have to wear underwear. Don't force your child to be potty trained. Instead, encourage her to take responsibility for her own training.

Put your child in cotton underwear during the day. If she has an accident, don't punish her or pressure her to use the potty. Instead, remind her of the household rule that big kids must have clean pants and make her change her underwear and help you clean up any messes she's made. Say nothing whatsoever about using the potty or toilet training. While this can be challenging, especially if your child is having frequent accidents, it returns control of potty training to her. The discomfort of frequently soiling her pants will force her to eventually begin using the potty. This approach works best when you have several days to spend at home with your child. The more time your child spends at home, the more opportunities she has to experience the discomfort of an accident and to see that she alone is responsible for her bodily functions.

Every time your child uses the potty, give her a reward. Emphasize that you are rewarding her for keeping her pants clean, not for using the potty. The key here is to remove all emphasis on potty training, because older kids are frequently so stressed by the potty training process that even mentioning potty training can cause them to regress.

Consistency is key with this system. You must be able to never put your child in diapers. If you are having company or leaving the house, put her in potty training pants to prevent messes. Avoid drawing attention to your child's potty training process, which can cause her to react defiantly. The only people who should know about the new household rules are your child's parents and any regular caregivers such as nannies or grandparents.

Many children this age are developing friendships and want to go on sleepovers or outings with friends. Without sounding angry or indicating that your child is being punished, remind her of the rule that big kids can't go out with dirty pants. Explain to her that, when she is able to keep her pants clean for several days, she'll be able to go to sleepovers and spend time with her friends away from her parents.

When your child has successfully completed potty training, lavish her with praise and treat her to a special present. Remind your child that he is being rewarded not for potty training, but for obeying the rule that big kids must keep their pants clean.

Potty Training Apps for the Android

Pull-Ups iGo Potty

Originally developed by the makers of Pull-Ups for the iPhone, this app is now available for androids. It features potty tracking charts and potty reminders for parents as well as interactive games for children. Parents can also play several potty sounds designed to help their children go while sitting on the toilet.

Once Upon a Potty

Based upon the beloved book, this app features editions for both boys and girls. This app features a narration of the original *Once Upon a Potty* as well as potty songs and games. Children sitting on the potty waiting to go will relate to the book's characters, who frequently wait and wait until they finally achieve potty training success.

Potty Training Basics

This app is designed to introduce parents to the process of potty training, and provides helpful overviews of several potty training methods. It features practical tips about how to incorporate potty training into a hectic schedule and how to avoid losing your temper when potty training becomes frustrating.

Potty Time

This comprehensive android app features potty trackers and charts for parents and songs, games and stories for children. Parents can give their children virtual stars and certificates for potty training achievements and print success charts to post on the refrigerator or wall. The app also features informative videos about potty training for parents and children to watch together.

Potty Stats

This app is designed to make tracking your child's potty achievements easy even on the go. It features potty tracking charts that not only help you track your child's progress but also help you predict when she might need to go next. It also provides a diaper savings chart pointing to how much money you have saved on diapers at every stage of potty training.

See Me Go Potty

This app makes it easy for your child to envision potty training success. Design an avatar that resembles your child and then let your child watch his avatar successfully use the potty. There is also a helpful tutorial about what an accident is and how to avoid them. Potty training tips for parents are also included.

iDump Toilet Training

While this app is unlikely to help you fully potty train your child, it is an excellent distraction for children sitting on the potty. Children can help little Tommy avoid distractions and effectively use the potty. This game puts a light-hearted spin on potty training and will have children eager to become potty trained and avoid distractions like Tommy.

Little Critter: The New Potty

The Little Critter stories have entertained generations of children, and The New Potty is an excellent introduction to potty training. This app features narration of the classic story. Little Sister must learn to use the potty and frequently makes mistakes, teaching children that accidents are ok. But Little Sister ultimately triumphs, mastering potty training and getting kids excited about learning.

Reward My Chore

Designed to reward children for completing any goal set by their parents, this app is perfect for setting up potty training milestones. Track your child's pottying progress and give her a thumbs up or gold star for good work. This modern alternative to the gold star chart allows you to reward your child anywhere while carefully charting his progress.

Parenting Tips

Featuring 24 videos on various parenting topics, this app includes several sections on potty training. Check out the checklist on potty training readiness, advice on what to do about bedwetting and how to help your child remain potty training even during times of stress and transitions to new caregivers.

Potty Training Apps for the iPhone

Joy Berry I Love Potty Training

Based upon Joy Berry's best-selling potty training books, this app is designed to be used by both children and their parents. It features potty training tips for parents, interactive potty training books for both girls and boys and potty training games. Parents can track their children's progress using the potty training tracker, and the program e-mails children a potty training diploma when they've successfully completed potty training.

Pull-Ups iGo Potty

Designed to make it easier for parents to track their children's potty schedule, this app is ideal for parents using the 15 minute method or who tend to forget to ask their child if she needs to go. Featuring a bright purple cartoon toilet, potty trackers and a countdown till your child's next visit to the bathroom, the bright colors and friendly design of this app will be appealing to children as well as their parents.

It's Potty Time

This app tells the story of a bunny called Bunni who is learning to use the potty. It includes a potty-themed song and information from Bunni about what it's like to use the potty. Parents may find the bunny a bit strange, but children will love singing along and celebrating Bunni's successes at using the potty.

Potty Chart

This app comes with a virtual chart that allows parents to give children virtual star stickers for potty training success. It includes several fun sound effects, including a few that reviewers swear help their children potty. It also has kid-friendly graphics, customizable potty trackers and separate pee and poop charts.

Potty Predictor

Ideal for parents using training methods that require them to predict their child's next trip to the bathroom, this app adjusts its predictions according to your child's actual potty schedule. Parents can also track food and drink intake, allowing them to track correlations between the things their children ingest and accidents. It also features accident and "potty try" trackers.

iPotty

This app is similar to other potty training tracking apps, with one significant difference: it's designed for kids to use themselves. It features an easily navigated screen from which children can track their own progress, give themselves gold stars for potty training success and learn more about the importance of being potty trained.

My Potty Chart

Similar to the Potty Chart app, this program features brighter colors and bigger pictures, with a screen that can be navigated by children themselves. There is no way to track non-success or accidents, which is appealing to parents who want to ensure they reward successes and simply deal with minor setbacks.

I Earned That

This is an excellent choice for parents using reward-based methods and who want to remind their child of the reward they'll get at the completion of potty training. Parents can take a picture of a reward for potty training and allow the app to break the photo into 60 jigsaw puzzle pieces. Every time your child successfully uses the potty, he gets another piece of the puzzle. When the entire picture appears, he gets a reward.

Huggies Potty Trainer

With features that appeal to both children and parents, this app allows you to select an avatar that represents your child. You can track your child's potty training progress and select potty sounds to help her go to the bathroom. It offers certificates for completion of potty training milestones and allows parents to set up potty reminders to help them remind their children to go to the bathroom.

Potty Panic

This app is not specifically designed to track potty training or provide rewards. Instead, it turns pottying into a fun game in which players have to make sure every character in the game gets to use the potty. A great distraction for kids sitting on the potty, it helps normalize the potty training process and reminds kids that even adults sometimes have trouble holding it in when they need to go!

Potty Training DVDs

For Children

Once Upon a Potty

This DVD tells the beloved story of a child learning to use the potty in simple language with anatomically correct illustrations. It comes in a version for boys with a main character named Joshua and version for girls with a main character named Prudence, making it easier for your child to relate to the toddler learning to use the potty.

Potty Power for Boys and Girls

Designed for children of both sexes, this DVD includes potty songs and dances. It aims to place potty training in a positive light and is especially useful for children who are resistant to or afraid of learning to use the potty. It also provides helpful tips to children about wiping and basic hygiene.

Sesame Street: Elmo's Potty Time

Featuring the beloved red monster, this DVD features Elmo, Baby Bear and Grover singing songs about potty training and discussing the importance of becoming a big kid. Elmo emphasizes that accidents are okay and that it takes a while to master potty training, a reassuring message for children anxious about the learning process.

I Can Go Potty

This DVD features an older sister narrating her brother's toilet training process. Children are encouraged to relate to both children and to want to become big kids who are fully potty trained. The story also provides information about how to wipe, how to raise and lower the seat and basic hygiene.

No More Diapers

In this story, a baby bear finds out that one of his friends doesn't wear diapers anymore. He decides he wants to be a big kid like his friend and begins potty training. The DVD walks viewers through the entire potty training process and is an ideal choice for parents who want their children to be excited about learning the new skill of using the potty.

Go Potty Go

This DVD, which has won several awards, features two animated panda bears learning to use the potty. There are several potty-related songs and stories, and characters emphasize to children the importance of hand washing and other basic hygiene tasks. The movie handles potty training in a light-hearted and fun manner that will get kids excited about the process.

For Parents and Children

The Magic Bowl: Potty Training Made Easy

Developed by child psychologist Dr. Baruch Kushnir, this DVD encourages children to use the toilet without first using a training potty. Although the DVD is designed to teach parents this potty training method, it is also an excellent resource for children. It features cartoon characters that treat the toilet as a warm, loving figure. This approach is ideal for children who have expressed fear about using the adult potty.

Bye Bye Diapers Potty Pack

This interactive DVD kit comes with a doll, storybook and a bear and is made in separate editions designed for girls and boys. It features songs, interactive games and child-friendly information about potty training. The DVD also provides parents with practical information and insights about the process of potty training.

Pull-Ups Big Kids Central Potty Training Success DVD

This DVD, designed for children at every phase of the potty training process, is available for free from Pull-Ups here (http://www.pull-ups.com/na/potty_training_dvd.aspx). It features potty training techniques and tips for parents as well as songs, stories and activities designed to make potty training more fun for children.

For Parents

Potty Training in One Day

This DVD showcases the popular one-day potty training method, making it an ideal choice for parents who don't have a lot of time to spend on potty training. Featuring practical tips, troubleshooting advice and information about the science of elimination, parents will come away from watching this video feeling fully equipped to institute the one day method.

Recommended Books that Discuss Potty Training

For Parents

The Everything Potty Training Book
by Linda Sonna

This book covers the potty training process from start to finish, including potty training readiness, ongoing accidents and bedwetting. Written in a non-academic tone for beginners, it devotes significant space to several different potty training methods. Parents who don't like committing to a specific method will find it especially helpful.

Toilet Training: A Practical Guide to Daytime and Nighttime Training by Vicki Lansky

While many potty training books treat toilet training as one item, this book recognizes the different struggles parents face in daytime and nighttime training. Filled with practical advice for managing accidents and dealing with uncooperative children, the book comes with a children's potty training book called *Koko Bear's New Potty*.

Mommy, I Have to Go Potty: A Parent's Guide to Toilet Training by Jan Faull

Among the most popular potty training guides for parents, this book features anecdotes from real parents and children that can help parents feel less alone. It addresses toilet training in other cultures, explains the importance of parents working together and offers troubleshooting advice for stubborn and fearful children.

Keys to Toilet Training by Meg Zweiback

Parents who dislike the cutesy language of many popular potty training books will find this book refreshing. Written by a pediatric nurse, it addresses both the physiology and psychology of potty training. It provides helpful tips for every phase of the potty training process as well as useful information about accidents, bedwetting and regression.

My Potty Activity Book by Tracy Foote

This book is a large activity book designed for parents and children to use together. Featuring potty training games, tracking charts and practical advice, it encourages children and parents to communicate openly with one another about potty training. It also features useful charts to help parents and children track toilet training progress.

For Children

Once Upon a Body by Alona Frankel

This classic book, first published in 1975, has helped generations of children master potty training. It features simple, anatomically correct illustrations ideal for very young children. The story narrates, from the child's perspective, the parts of the body used in potty training and the potty training process.

Going to the Potty by Fred Rogers

Written by the beloved Mr. Rogers, this book features a diverse group of real children using the potty. It does not show the children naked, but does frankly discuss bodily functions and the process of using the toilet. Potty training is portrayed in a positive light, and Rogers emphasizes that making mistakes is part of the learning process.

Everyone Poops by Tara Gomi and Amanda Mayer Stinchecum

This light-hearted look at the bowel functions of numerous animals normalizes the process of pooping. It features simple, sometimes funny illustrations and commentary on the ways in which various species poop. It is an excellent choice for shy parents and children because it turns pooping into a normal -- and occasionally funny – act.

Potty by Leslie Patricelli

This board book is an excellent choice for very young toddlers who are only beginning to learn about the process of elimination. It features an adorable baby contemplating the value of using the potty versus going in his diaper. Light-hearted in tone, the book concludes with the baby finally mastering using the potty.

Potty Time With Elmo by Publication International

Featuring Elmo, the perennial Sesame Street favorite, this book is highly interactive and allows children to push buttons to make potty sounds. An excellent choice for getting kids used to the sounds and sights of using the toilet, it features Elmo potty training his doll. The book provides little information about the actual process of using the potty, but is a good primer for making potty training seem fun.

Conclusion

For as long as there have been parents and children, parents have struggled with potty training their children. Potty training is the first time in your child's life he has to actively exert control over his own body, and when he's completed this important milestone, it's important to celebrate his very first step toward independence. While potty training can be challenging, remember that there aren't many stories about adults who are not potty trained! Ignore advice from well-meaning friends and family if it doesn't jive with your intuitions. Use the time spent potty training to work together with your child to achieve a shared goal. This is a powerful opportunity for both you and your child to practice communication and teamwork. You'll get there, one way or another, and you and your child can become closer in the process.

About Minute Help Press

Minute Help Press is building a library of books for people with only minutes to spare. Follow @minutehelp on Twitter to receive the latest information about free and paid publications from Minute Help Press, or visit minutehelpguides.com.

Sources:

Rogoff, B. (2003). *The cultural nature of human development*. Oxford: Oxford University Press.